# Uniquely
# Nevada

Rebecca K. O'Connor and Dennis Myers

**Heinemann Library**
Chicago, Illinois

Designed by Heinemann Library
Printed in China by WKT Company Limited.

08 07 06 05 04
10 9 8 7 6 5 4 3 2 1

**Library of Congress
Cataloging-in-Publication Data**

O'Connor, Rebecca.
  Uniquely Nevada / Rebecca K. O'Connor and Dennis Myers.
    v. cm.
Includes bibliographical references and index.
Contents: Uniquely Nevada—Nevada's geography and climate—Famous firsts—Nevada state symbols—Nevada's history & people—Las vegas—Nevada's state government—Nevada's culture—Nevada's food—Nevada's folklore and legends—Nevada's sports teams—Nevada's businesses and products—Attractions and landmarks.
  ISBN 1-4034-4650-4 (lib. bdg.)—
  ISBN 1-4034-4719-5 (pbk.)
  1. Nevada—Juvenile literature. [1. Nevada.]
    I. Myers, Dennis. II. Title.
  F841.3.O28 2004
  979.3'034—dc22
                                    2003025718

**Cover Pictures**

**Top** (left to right) Nevada ghost town, Welcome to Las Vegas sign, Nevada state flag, Death Valley National Park
**Main** Aerial view of the Hoover Dam

**Acknowledgments**
Development and photo research by
BOOK BUILDERS LLC

The author and publishers are grateful to the following for permission to reproduce copyrighted material: Cover photographs by (top, L-R):  Layne Kennedy/Corbis; Owaki-Kulla/Corbis; Joe Sohm/ Alamy; W. Wayne Lockwood, M.D./Corbis; (main): Corbis. Title page (L-R): EuroStyle Graphics/Alamy; W.K. Fletcher/Photo Researchers; Nevada Commission on Tourism; Contents page: Stephen Saks Photography/Alamy; p. 5 Owaki-Kulla/Corbis; p. 6 W. Wayne Lockwood, M.D./Corbis; p. 7, 40, 45 IMA for BOOK BUILDERS LLC; p. 8 Courtesy Levi Strauss & Co. Archives; p. 9 Corbis; p. 10T Joe Sohm/Alamy; p. 10B One Mile Up; p. 11T  eStock; p. 11B Gregory Dimijian/Photo Researchers, Inc.; p. 12T U.S. Fish and Wildlife Service/photo by Dave Menke; p. 12M Dave Powell/USDA Forestry Service; p. 12B U.S. Fish and Wildlife Service/ photo by Peter J. Carboni; p. 13T U.S. Fish and Wildlife Service/photo by Robert W. Hines; p. 13M U.S. Fish and Wildlife Service/photo by Beth Jackson; p. 13B, 24, 26B, 35, 37, 39T, 44 Nevada Commission on Tourism; p. 14T Stock Montage, Inc./Alamy; p. 14B, 21, 27 Original work the property of the University of Nevada-Las Vegas; p. 15T Courtesy of AZ Rock Shop; p. 15B Richard T. Nowitz/Photo Researchers, Inc.; p. 16 W.K. Fletcher/Photo Researchers, Inc.; p. 17, 18 Culver; p. 20T University of Nevada Special Collections, University of Nevada-Reno Library; p. 20B Popperfoto/Alamy; p. 22T, 22B EuroStyle Graphics/Alamy; p. 25 Courtesy of the Reno-Sparks Convention and Visitors Authority; p. 26T Layne Kennedy/Corbis; p. 29 Batista Moon Studio/ Alamy; p. 31 Thomas Hallstein/Alamy; p. 32, 33, 34 Russell Wright; p. 39B Courtesy of Fort Churchill State Historic Park; p. 41 Stephen Saks Photography/Alamy; p. 42 Photo 24/Alamy.

Special thanks to Guy Louis Rocha of the Nevada State Library and Archives for his expert comments in the preparation of this book.

Every effort has been made to contact copyright holders of any material reproduced in this book. Any omissions will be rectified in subsequent printings if notice is given to the publisher.

Some words are shown in bold, **like this.** You can find out what they mean by looking in the glossary.

# Contents

# Uniquely Nevada

**U**nique means one of a kind. Nevada is unique in many ways. For example, Nevada's population is growing faster than that of any other state. Nevada is the driest state in the country. The world's oldest trees are also found in Nevada. Nevada's geography, people, and history have made it a one of a kind place.

Nevada is located in the western part of the United States. It is bordered by Oregon and Idaho on the north and by California on the south and west. To the east, Nevada is bordered by Utah and Arizona. Nevada is the seventh-largest state in the country, but it ranks 39th in population.

## Origin of The State's Name

Nevada is named after the Sierra Nevada mountain range that is shared by Nevada and California. *Nevada* is a Spanish word meaning "snow" or "snowy"; and *sierra* means "mountains."

## Major Cities

Nevada is one of the five most urban states in the nation. Thus, most people live in the state's cities rather than in the country or in rural areas.

The capital of Nevada, Carson City, has a population of more than 52,000. For many years, it was known as the capital with the smallest population in the nation. But Nevada's population is growing so rapidly that now twelve other states have capital cities with smaller populations. The Capitol, or state building, was built between 1870 and 1871. Many of the neighborhoods in the city are old and picturesque, and so are the homes. Carson City also has another distinction. It is one of very few communities around the nation that is not inside a county but stands alone as an independent city.

Las Vegas, with a population of more than 500,000, is the largest city in Nevada. Located at the southern tip of the state, Las Vegas was once a small, quiet town, but today it is one of the most famous cities in the world. Huge hotels and casinos have made Las Vegas a major vacation destination. More than 32 million people vacation in Las Vegas each year.

*This historic sign welcomes visitors driving into the city on Las Vegas Boulevard, or "the Strip."*

Reno, with a population of about 180,000, is the largest city in northern Nevada. It began as a river crossing and grew into a railroad town. It is home to one of the largest automobile collections in the nation. The University of Nevada, Reno, looks so much like an old-fashioned campus that Hollywood directors have often used it in movies.

# Nevada's Geography and Climate

**S**andy deserts, snow-covered mountains with forested slopes, and grassy valleys are all part of Nevada's landscape. The state is divided into three main land regions—the Columbia Plateau, the Sierra Nevada, and the Basin and Range Region.

*Death Valley National Park in the Basin and Range Region is one of the hottest places in the United States.*

## LAND

The Columbia Plateau covers the northeastern corner of Nevada, which is made up of **lava** bedrock. Rivers and streams have cut deeply into the bedrock, leaving deep canyons with steep ridges. The land becomes open prairie in the north, near the Idaho border.

The Sierra Nevada is a rugged mountain range that cuts across Nevada south of Carson City. Lake Tahoe, a lake formed by **glaciers** thousands of years ago, lies in one of the valleys of the Sierra Nevada. The lake is located on the California-Nevada border.

The rest of the state is called the Basin and Range Region, which is divided by more than 150 mountain ranges running north to south. Scattered between the ranges are **buttes** and **mesas** as well as valleys with lakes and **salt flats.**

## CLIMATE

Nevada is the driest state in the country. Most of the state receives an average of four inches of **precipitation** each year because the state lies in the **rain shadow** of the Sierra Nevada. On summer days, temperatures often soar to more than 100°F, but may drop to between 40°F and 50°F at night. Winter's daytime temperatures are usually pleasant, reaching 60°F to 70°F, but can be much cooler at night. Temperatures in the mountains are generally cooler.

## Hot Springs in Nevada

The earth's crust in the Great Basin is very thin. Just below the crust is a layer of melted rock. Ground water lying beneath the Great Basin is heated by this molten rock and bubbles to the surface through cracks in the earth's crust. Nevada has more than 300 of these pools of hot water, called hot springs.

*The highest concentration of precipitation in the state is in the Carson City/Lake Tahoe area.*

## Average Annual Precipitation
## Nevada

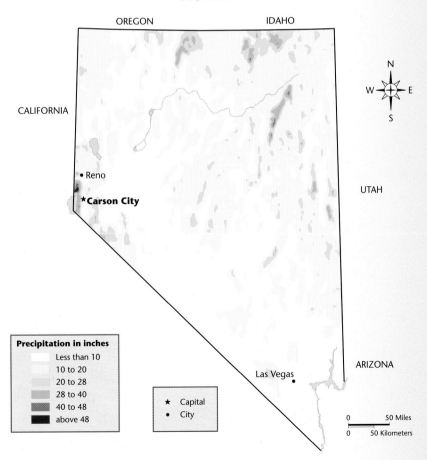

**Precipitation in inches**
- Less than 10
- 10 to 20
- 20 to 28
- 28 to 40
- 40 to 48
- above 48

★ Capital
• City

0        50 Miles

0      50 Kilometers

# Famous Firsts

*Davis and Strauss called their new pants, waist overalls.*

### INVENTION FIRSTS

Jacob Davis, a Nevada tailor, developed the idea of using copper rivets at the stress points in work pants. He approached Levi Strauss, a successful San Francisco businessman, with the idea, and they obtained a patent for it. The blue jeans they developed were extremely durable—an important feature for hard-working miners—and a great improvement over other work pants.

### EDUCATION FIRSTS

The University of Nevada is the only U.S. university offering a doctoral degree in **Basque** Studies. It offers one of only three Basque Studies programs in the world.

### WOMEN'S FIRSTS

Anne Martin of Nevada was the first woman to run for the U.S. Senate. She first tried for the office in 1918, ran again in 1920, but lost both times.

Barbara Vucanovich was the first woman to be elected to a federal office from Nevada. She was elected in November 1982 to serve Nevada's 2nd District in Congress and was reelected to each succeeding Congress until her retirement in 1996. As Republican Conference Secretary for the 104th Congress, she was the first Nevadan to serve in a leadership position in the U.S. House of Representatives.

According to the 2000 United States **census,** 1,998,257 people live in Nevada. In the 1990 census, Nevada's population was 1,201,833. Nevada had the largest population increase of any state in the United States—66.3 percent.

## NATURE FIRSTS

Nevada is the only state to possess a complete skeleton of an ichthyosaur (See p. 13). The skeleton is about 55 feet long. This reptile swam in the waters that covered Nevada before people lived there million of years ago.

Pyramid Lake is home to the cui-ui fish. This fish can be found nowhere else in the world, because it has never found its way to any other habitat. The Devil's Hole pupfish lives in a hot water pool in a small cavern. This is also the only place it lives.

## INNOVATION FIRSTS

The building of the Hoover Dam in the early 1930s was a modern marvel. It was the largest government project in the United States up to that time, and it has been called "the architectural masterpiece among all the world's dams." One of the largest concrete dams in the world, it is a **hydroelectric** dam, and produces electricity for Nevada, California, and Arizona.

*Hoover Dam is 726.4 feet tall from its foundation to the roadway at the top.*

# Nevada's State Symbols

*Nevada's state flag was adopted in 1927 and changed slightly in 1991.*

*The state seal shows the importance of silver and gold mining to the state.*

### NEVADA STATE FLAG

On the Nevada flag are two branches of sagebrush, the state flower. A banner above the sagebrush reads "Battle Born" because Nevada became a state during the **Civil War** (1861–1865).

### STATE SEAL

The state seal of Nevada, adopted in 1866, features a ring of 36 stars because Nevada was the 36th state admitted to the Union. Images inside the ring of stars show important parts of Nevada history. The large railroad **trestle,** which did not yet exist in Nevada when the seal was adopted, showed confidence in the state's future. Nevada's agriculture is represented by a sheaf, or bundle, of wheat, a **sickle,** and a plow.

### NEVADA STATE MOTTO: "ALL FOR OUR COUNTRY"

The state motto, "All For Our Country," expresses the state's loyalty to the United States during the Civil War. It was adopted in 1864.

### STATE NICKNAME: "SILVER STATE"

Nevada's nickname is the "Silver State" because silver mining was important to the state's early history.

## "Home Means Nevada"

Way out in the land of the
   setting sun,
Where the wind blows wild and free,
There's a lovely spot, just the only one
That means home sweet home to me.
If you follow the old Kit Carson trail,
Until desert meets the hills,
Oh you certainly will agree with me,
It's the place of a thousand thrills.

**Chorus**
Home means Nevada,
Home means the hills,
Home means the sage and the pines.
Out by the Truckee's silvery rills,
Out where the sun always shines,
Here is the land that I love the best,
Fairer than all I can see.
Deep in the heart of the golden west
Home means Nevada to me.

### STATE SONG: "HOME MEANS NEVADA"

Bertha Raffetto wrote "Home Means Nevada" over a period of years. She completed it for the 1932 Nevada Native Daughters group picnic. It was so well liked, within a year, it became the state song of Nevada.

### STATE FLOWER: SAGEBRUSH

State lawmakers made sagebrush Nevada's state flower in 1959. A common plant in the Great Basin and many parts of the west, it was important to Native Americans for medicine. It is also considered an indicator of fertile soil in dry areas.

*Sagebrush is known for its yellow flowers.*

### STATE TREES: PINION PINE AND BRISTLECONE PINE

Nevada has two state trees. The single leaf pinion became a state tree in 1953. The bristlecone pine is the oldest living tree on earth. It grows on high mountains in Great Basin National Park. It was named a state tree in 1987.

*The single-leaf pinion produces pine nuts, which were an important food for early Native Americans and pioneers.*

*The mountain bluebird is migratory and can be found all over the west.*

### STATE BIRD: MOUNTAIN BLUEBIRD

The mountain bluebird became the state bird in 1967. It lives in the Nevada high country and eats harmful insects. A member of the thrush family, its song is a clear, short warble. The male is deep blue with a white belly, while the female is brown with a bluish rump, tail, and wings.

### STATE GRASS: INDIAN RICE GRASS

Indian rice grass grows fast and spreads quickly, which helps restore the land after range fires. That is one of the reasons the Nevada Legislature chose the plant to be the state grass in 1977. Native Americans who lived in the Great Basin used Indian rice grass as grain. They ground it into meal to bake bread.

*In summer, Indian Rice grass turns straw color.*

### STATE ANIMAL: DESERT BIGHORN SHEEP

The desert bighorn sheep became the state animal in 1973. It can survive without water in the winter if green vegetation is available to eat. In summer, however, they must find water at least every three days.

*The desert bighorn's hooves help it run up rocky hillsides.*

## STATE FISH: LAHONTAN CUTTHROAT TROUT

The Lahontan cutthroat trout was named the state fish in 1981. The trout was chosen as the state fish in part for its economic and historic importance. In the late 1800s, tons of the trout from the Pyramid Lake Paiute Tribal Reservation were shipped to mining camps to feed miners during the gold and silver booms.

*Lahonton cutthroats get their name from red colored slashes under their jaws.*

## STATE REPTILE: DESERT TORTOISE

The desert tortoise lives to be around 70 years old. It is usually found in the far southern part of Nevada. The legislature named the tortoise Nevada's state reptile in 1989.

## STATE FOSSIL: ICHTHYOSAUR

The ichthyosaur, a prehistoric fish-like reptile, ranged from 50 to 60 feet in length and weighed about 50 tons. Like today's reptiles, it breathed air. It became the state fossil in 1977.

*The desert tortoise is the largest reptile in the Southwestern United States.*

*Many ichthyosaur fossils have been discovered at Berlin—Ichthyosaur State Park.*

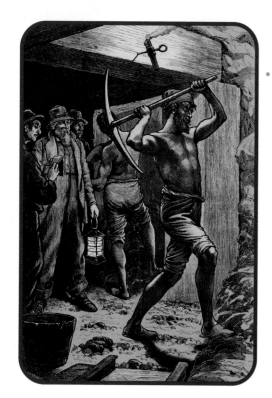

*One of the biggest lodes of silver in the world was found in Nevada.*

### STATE METAL: SILVER

Silver is one of the most important minerals in Nevada's history. Legislators made it the state metal in 1977, more than a century after it was discovered in Nevada.

### STATE ROCK: SANDSTONE

Sandstone, also called quartzite, is a part of Nevada's scenery and is also used to construct buildings. The state capitol and the former U.S. Mint building in Carson City are built from sandstone. The legislature designated sandstone the state rock in 1987.

*Sandstone is found throughout Nevada. Spectacular sandstone formations at Valley of Fire State Park and Red Rock Canyon National Conservation Area are favorite vacation destinations.*

## STATE PRECIOUS GEMSTONE: VIRGIN VALLEY BLACK FIRE OPAL

Nevada adopted the black fire opal as its state precious gemstone in 1987. Nevada's Virgin Valley is the only place in North America where large quantities of these opals are found. The black fire opal is a highly valued gemstone. They can be more valuable than diamonds, but they are very fragile and thus are not good for use in jewelry. Opals instead are often displayed in water. Opals refract light very well and shine with bursts of multi-colored light.

*The Virgin Valley black fire opals are often found on fossilized wood.*

## STATE SEMIPRECIOUS GEMSTONE: TURQUOISE

Turquoise, a stone that ranges in color from light blue to dark green, became the state's official semiprecious gemstone in 1987. Native Americans first used the gem to make jewelry, and it is still a popular gemstone today.

*Turquoise is sometimes called the jewel of the desert.*

# Nevada's History and People

**N**evada's history has been influenced by the state's rugged land and desert conditions. Having very few natural resources besides minerals, the region was a hard place for people to make a home. Nevada's population grew slowly.

### NEVADA'S FIRST PEOPLE

Little is known about the first people to live in the Great Basin about 11,000 years ago. During the **Paleolithic** era, or Old Stone Age, they lived in caves around Lake Lahontan, a large lake that covered much of what is Nevada today, and near Lake Las Vegas, and hunted large mammals.

More than 2,300 years ago, after the region's climate had become desert-like, a new group of people called the Anasazi arrived in the Great Basin. They lived in pueblos, multi-room structures where whole communities

*The Great Basin's dry climate made it difficult to grow crops, yet the Anasazi flourished for over 1,000 years.*

lived together. The Anasazi developed their skills rapidly, creating tools, making pottery, fishing, mining, and farming. They also developed an irrigation system—diverting river water into channels to supply their crops. One of their communities, Pueblo Grande de Nevada, was excavated and is now the subject of the Lost City Museum at Lake Mead. It displays Anasazi tools, dwellings, and other objects illustrating the Anasazi way of life. The Anasazi civilization disappeared quickly around 1215, for reasons that are unknown.

A number of tribes of Native Americans—the Northern Paiute, the Washo, the Owens Valley Paiute, the Western Shoshone, and the Southern Paiute—moved into the Great Basin after the Anasazi disappeared. In the northern and central Great Basin, the people tended to gather foods already growing there, while the people in the southern basin planted crops such as squash and beans, and gathered food as well. Because of the harsh desert conditions, many of Nevada's first people were nomadic, moving from place to place in search of water and better living conditions.

## EARLY EXPLORERS

In 1826–1827, a party of fifteen men led by Jedediah Smith of the Rocky Mountain Fur Company traveled through the Great Basin. These were the first white explorers to enter Nevada. In 1830, Antonio Armijo and a large party of Mexicans traveled through southern Nevada. His scout, Rafael Rivera, may have been the first non-Native American to set foot in the Las Vegas Valley. These two parties provided information for later explorers. Because of the harsh, dry conditions, few white settlers moved to the area. Later, after the discovery of silver and gold, prospectors and miners would flock to the region to become rich.

*Jedediah Smith narrowly escaped death at the hands of the Mohave tribe during his trapping expedition in Nevada.*

## Part of Mexico, 1821–1848

The land that is today called the American Southwest, which includes present-day Nevada, was claimed by Spain until 1821. In that year, Mexico won its independence from Spain, and ownership of the land that is present-day Nevada passed to Mexico.

While Nevada belonged to Mexico, explorers from the United States, such as John C. Frémont, traveled through the territory, mapping the area. Frémont named Pyramid Lake, a remnant of ancient Lake Lahontan, and many of the area's other lakes and mountains.

In 1846, war broke out between Mexico and the United States. With the signing of the Treaty of Guadalupe Hidalgo in 1848, the war ended. Mexico **ceded** about one-third of its land to the United States. This huge tract of land included the present-day states of California, Nevada, and Utah, and parts of Arizona, New Mexico, Colorado, and Wyoming.

## A United States Territory

Few white settlers lived in Nevada when it became part of the United States. However, with the discovery of gold in California in 1848, more people traveled across Nevada to get to the gold mines. Some of them stopped and stayed in Nevada to seek their fortunes. These **prospectors** traveled along Nevada's rivers looking for gold and silver.

*Mining was hard work for the prospectors, but the rewards made thousands of people search for gold and silver in Nevada.*

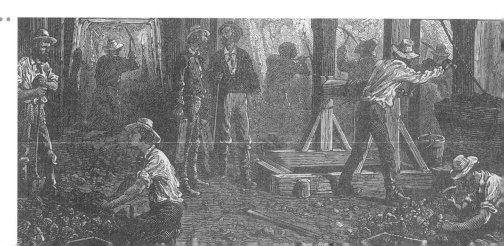

In 1857, two gold prospectors from Pennsylvania discovered one of the largest silver strikes in the world, the Comstock Lode. Because of this discovery, many people came to the area, hoping to make their fortune. The silver they discovered brought wealth and even more people to Nevada. By 1861, more than 14,000 people had settled in the region. In March 1861, the U.S. Congress officially created the Nevada Territory.

## STATEHOOD

On October 31, 1864, Nevada became the 36th state in the Union. Today, that date is a state holiday, Nevada Day. President Abraham Lincoln wanted Nevada to become a state because he believed its representatives in Congress would likely support his plans for **Reconstruction** after the Civil War. Soon after becoming a state, Nevada **ratified** the Thirteenth Amendment (1865) outlawing slavery, the Fourteenth Amendment (1868) protecting civil rights, and the Fifteenth Amendment (1870) guaranteeing all men the right to vote.

## FAMOUS PEOPLE FROM NEVADA

**Dat So La Lee** (1829–1925), artist, basketweaver. Lee, a Washo tribe member, was born in the Carson Valley. She wove degikup baskets, the kind of baskets Native Americans in the Great Basin and California had been making for centuries. The baskets, which were made from natural materials such as willow twigs and tule reeds, are now highly prized and displayed in museums.

**Sarah Winnemucca Hopkins** (1844–1891), author, interpreter, and activist. Hopkins, a Native American, was born near the Humboldt River. Her Paiute name was Thocmetony. She worked for peace between the settlers and Pauite in Nevada. She wrote a book about her life—the first autobiography ever written by a Native American woman. The Nevada Women's History Project has commissioned a statue of her, which will be placed in Statuary Hall in the United States Capitol in Washington, D.C.

**Wovoka** (1858?–1932), religious leader. Wovoka, a Paiute, was born in Carson County, Utah Territory, which later became Esmeralda County in Nevada. A **prophet,** Wovoka claimed that in the future whites would disappear from the earth and all Native Americans, living and dead, would live on the land again. They would be free from death, disease, and misery. His teachings swept across the United States, influencing tribes throughout the west and the Great Plains.

**Eva Adams** (1908–1991), political aide, agency director. Adams was born in Wonder, a mining camp. After graduating from the University of Nevada, she attended Columbia University in New York City. She later became an aide to Nevada Senator Pat McCarran. In 1961, President John F. Kennedy named her Director of the U.S. Mint, where she served until 1969.

**Walter Van Tilburg Clark** (1909–1971), poet, novelist. Clark grew up in Nevada and taught at the University of Nevada in Reno. His books *The Track of the Cat* and *The Ox-Bow Incident* are classics that were both made into movies.

**Paul Laxalt** (1922– ), politician, real estate developer. Laxalt was born in Carson City, and served as Nevada's lieutenant governor, governor, and U.S. senator. He was the first person of **Basque** heritage to be elected to those offices.

**Andre Agassi** (1970– ), tennis player. Agassi, who was born in Las Vegas, won a gold medal in tennis for the United States at the 1996 Olympics. He has also won eight grand slam tournaments, the major tennis events in four different nations—the United States, Australia, France, and the United Kingdom.

*Walter Van Tilburg Clark's books are steeped in the lore of Nevada.*

*Andre Agassi is one of the most sucessful and popular champions in tennis history.*

# Las Vegas

In the second half of the 1900s, Nevada became one of the nation's major tourist destinations. The population of the state shifted from northern Nevada to southern Nevada, especially around the Las Vegas area.

## GAMBLING LEGALIZED—1931

In 1931, gambling became legal in Nevada. Legal gambling led to the construction of large casinos, attracting visitors from out of state. Casinos, construction on the Hoover Dam, and railroad work brought many people to Las Vegas.

The first hotel and casino, El Rancho Vegas, grew successful by providing both gambling and entertainment. Its success encouraged the construction of other resorts on U.S. 91 by people eager to attract tourists, especially visitors from southern California. This road reached from Los Angeles to Las Vegas. In Las Vegas, the stretch of road with hotels and casinos became known as the Strip.

El Rancho Vegas was built in 1941. A huge fire caused it to close down in 1960.

## GROWTH IN THE 1950S

In the 1950s, more resorts were built. Air travel became more popular, and tourists came to gamble during the day and see the entertainers who performed at the resorts every night. Many popular singers, comedians, and dancers entertained hotel guests.

*The nine-story Riviera Hotel, the first high-rise on the Strip, had a panoramic view of Las Vegas in 1955.*

For example, Elvis Presley, Dean Martin, Jerry Lewis, Liberace, Juliet Prowse, and Frank Sinatra appeared on the hotel stages. In the 1960s, Nevada law was changed to allow companies, as well as individuals, to have casino licenses. This change allowed big companies to invest in huge hotels known as mega-resorts. Las Vegas has continued to grow at a rapid pace ever since.

### FAMILY FUN AND TOURISM TODAY

Today, Las Vegas remains one of the most popular tourist destinations in the country. For example, in 2002, about 35,100,000 tourists visited Las Vegas. Casinos and shows remain the biggest adult attraction. Families, however, travel to the area to visit Hoover Dam, the Valley of Fire, the Lost City Museum, Red Rock Canyon, and other attractions. Some casinos, too, are providing fun for the whole family by adding rides and roller coasters.

## Travel the World in Las Vegas

A trip down the Las Vegas Strip can be a trip around the world. Many of the mega-resorts are built around themes involving distant places. The Paris Las Vegas Hotel includes a model of the famous Eiffel Tower found in Paris, France. At the Luxor, tourists can stay in a pyramid resembling those built in ancient Egypt. The New York, New York, resort includes a roller coaster whose passenger cars look like New York City taxicabs.

# Nevada's State Government

**N**evada's government is based in Carson City, the capital. Similar to the **federal government** in Washington, D.C., Nevada's government is made up of three branches—the legislative branch, the executive branch, and the judicial branch.

## THE LEGISLATIVE BRANCH

Nevada's legislature makes the state's laws. It consists of two houses—the senate and the assembly. The senate's 21 members are elected to 4-year terms and are limited to 3 terms. The assembly's 42 members are elected to 2-year terms and are limited to 6 terms.

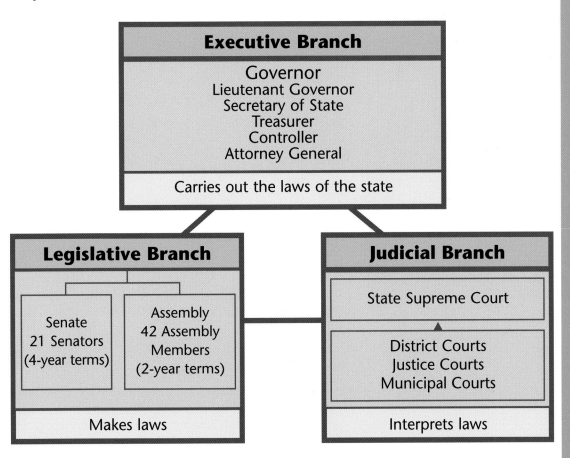

**Executive Branch**

Governor
Lieutenant Governor
Secretary of State
Treasurer
Controller
Attorney General

Carries out the laws of the state

**Legislative Branch**

Senate
21 Senators
(4-year terms)

Assembly
42 Assembly
Members
(2-year terms)

Makes laws

**Judicial Branch**

State Supreme Court

District Courts
Justice Courts
Municipal Courts

Interprets laws

A bill, or proposed law, may start in either house of the legislature. A bill must be approved by a **majority** of the members of both houses before it can be sent to the governor for approval. If the governor signs the bill, it becomes a law. If the governor **vetoes** the bill, it does not become a law. However, a two-thirds majority of the legislature may override the governor's veto.

## THE EXECUTIVE BRANCH

The executive branch enforces the laws and runs the state from day to day. The governor is the head of this branch. Voters elect the governor to a four-year term of office. The governor is limited to two four-year terms. Other elected executive officials are the lieutenant governor, the secretary of state, the treasurer, the controller, and the attorney general.

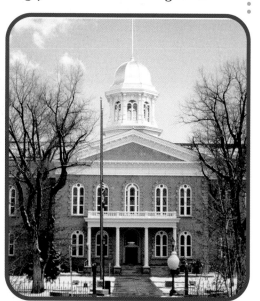

*Completed in 1870, the capitol was the tallest building in Carson City for more than 100 years.*

## THE JUDICIAL BRANCH

The judicial branch interprets Nevada's laws. There are four courts in Nevada's judicial system. The municipal courts hear minor cases, such as those having to do with traffic laws. The justice courts handle minor crimes and **civil** matters that involve less than $7,500. The district courts rule over **criminal,** civil, family, and juvenile disputes. These courts also hear **appeals** from justice courts and municipal courts. The Supreme Court is the state's highest court. Its chief responsibility is to review appeals from district court cases. The Supreme Court has seven elected justices, and the justice with the greatest seniority serves as chief justice.

# Nevada's Culture

**N**evada's cultural events celebrate the diversity of the people who live in the state. From festivals honoring the Native American and **Basque** cultures to celebrations of the cowboy and mining cultures of the Old West, Nevada recognizes all the elements of the state's heritage.

## NATIVE AMERICAN HERITAGE

Before the arrival of Europeans in the 1800s, Native Americans—Paiute, Washo, and Shoshone tribes—lived in what is present-day Nevada. Today, these Native American groups proudly commemorate their cultural heritage, passing down their traditions to each generation, while sharing them with others through celebrations called powwows. In a festival-like setting, powwows honor Native American elders and memorialize past leaders. Powwows also sometimes pay tribute to Native American war veterans and special tribal members such as mothers and grandmothers.

Powwows highlight Native American skills and talents through dance, music, food, and art.

## THE HERITAGE OF THE OLD WEST

After the Comstock Lode was discovered, prospectors flooded the territory looking for gold and silver. In a short time, small mines dotted the area, but once the minerals were removed, the prospectors moved on, looking for new mineral reserves to mine. Towns had sprung up around the mines, providing places for the miners to

*The abandoned buildings are the only evidence that these remote settlements were once successful towns.*

cash in their gold and silver nuggets or trade their wealth for tools and equipment. But once the miners left, so did the people in the towns. These settlements became **ghost towns.**

Most ghost towns are abandoned, but a few communities whose mines have long since closed, such as Midas and Goldfield, are not deserted. Each year, for example, thousands of tourists from all over the world visit places like Virginia City, where they can wander through well-preserved mansions, churches, and inns to see what life was like more than a century ago. The Old West is an important part of the state's heritage.

## NEVADA FESTIVALS

Each July, in Elko, the Basque people hold the National Basque Festival. The Basques are from the mountainous area along the Spanish-French border in Europe. Many Basques came to the United States in the late 1800s and settled in the west. Today, there are about 300,000 people of Basque descent in the United States. At the festival, Basque children perform native dances in colorful costumes. Adults, too, dance to the music of their ancestors and challenge each other in competitions such as weightlifting, wood chopping, and bread making.

*The Elko Arinak Basque Dancers are a group of Basque people who preform traditional dances at festivals throughout the region.*

Each Labor Day weekend, the town of Fallon holds the Cantaloupe Festival because the area is well known for Hearts of Gold, an especially tasty cantaloupe. Visitors enjoy cantaloupe-eating contests, shop the market of locally grown produce, and watch a children's **rodeo.** About 20,000 people attend the Cantaloupe Festival each year.

Elko County has held a Cowboy Poetry Gathering every January since 1984. Cowhands tell stories and rhymes, and the festival has gained nationwide recognition. Perhaps the festival is one reason why Elko is known as "the last real cowboy town in America." About 8,000 people attend the event.

The Clark County Rodeo is a professional rodeo where many people come to compete and watch. At rodeos, cowhands demonstrate their skill at riding horses and moving cattle. The Clark County rodeo keeps alive the spirit of the Old West and allows visitors to experience the tough life of cattle hands.

*Ranches like the Dressler Ranch were important parts of Nevada's Old West culture.*

The National Championship Air Races, in Reno, attracts airplane fans from all over the world. First held in 1964 at the former Reno Army Air Base, visitors can see aerobatic performers and aviation displays. Planes compete by type, such as jet, biplane, or sport. Planes race in courses as long as eight miles in the air, in which the plane that flies the fastest wins the race. The race is the fastest motor sport in the world. In 1996, a single-engine P-51 Mustang airplane from the 1940s flew at a speed greater than 375 mph.

# Nevada's Food

**N**evada's food reflects the state's diverse heritage. Today, visitors can find almost any type of food in Nevada's many restaurants.

## BEEF

Nevada has more than one-half million head of beef cattle on huge ranches throughout the state. The state's cattle-ranching traditions and the foods produced from them date back to the late 1800s. Today, beef remains a favorite of many Nevadans, and can be found in dishes such as Nevada Cowboy Chili.

## BASQUE TRADITIONS

Unique to Nevada are its many **Basque** restaurants. Found in cities and towns such as Gardnerville, Elko, Reno, and Winnemucca, the restaurants are gathering places for the Basque community—although everyone is welcome. Diners eat around long community tables where they can meet and talk to one another. "This is the way we serve meals in the old country. Everybody sits together, eats good food, and becomes friends after a while. This common dining is one of the Basque traditions that visitors often come to sample," notes one Basque restaurant owner. Fish and seafood dishes are Basque favorites. Chorizo, a spicy sausage, and lentils are also used in many Basque dishes.

# Nevada Cowboy Chili

**Ask an adult to help you with this recipe.**

1/2 cup lard or vegetable shortening

3 medium onions, coarsely chopped

2 bell peppers coarsely chopped

2 celery stalks, coarsely chopped

1 tablespoon pickled jalapeno peppers

8 pounds ground beef

1 can (30 ounces) stewed tomatoes

1 can (15 ounces) tomato sauce

1 can (6 ounces) tomato paste

8 tablespoons ground red hot chili

4 tablespoons ground red mild chili

2 teaspoons ground cumin

3 bay leaves

1 tablespoon liquid hot pepper sauce

garlic salt to taste

onion salt to taste

salt to taste

fresh ground black pepper

water

Melt the lard in a large heavy pot over medium high heat. Add the onions, peppers, celery, and jalapenos. Cook, stirring, until the onions are clear. Add the meat to the pot. Break up any lumps with a fork and cook, stirring occasionally, until the meat is evenly browned. Stir in the remaining ingredients with enough water to cover. Bring to a boil, and then lower the heat and simmer, uncovered, for three hours. Stir often. Taste and adjust seasonings.

# Nevada's Folklore and Legends

Legends and folklore are stories that are not totally true, but are often based on bits of truth. These stories helped people understand things that could not be easily explained. They also taught lessons to—and entertained—younger generations. All peoples have passed down stories as part of their culture.

## THE INVISIBLE HANDS

Many years ago two **Welsh** miners came to Nevada to help mine the Comstock Lode. They were both big pranksters and, after a while, no one would believe anything they said. One evening the two Welshmen were working late, and when they stopped for a break, they heard voices and the sound of hammers striking a drill.

The Welshmen followed the sound of the hammers and came into a shaft lit by a single lantern. The Welshmen were shocked! Two hammers, floating in mid-air, were striking the head of a rusty old drill that was rotating by itself. They could hear a murmur of voices but could see no one.

With a frightened yell, the Welshmen ran out of the mine and told their shocking story to some of their friends. But no one would believe them, thinking it was just another practical joke.

Finally, the Welshmen took two of their fellow workers to the mine. When the four men entered the shaft, the invisible hands were still hard at work. "It's the bucca!" shouted one of the workers, who had come to Nevada from England. The bucca were small **imps** who lived in mines. The miners ran out of the shaft as fast as they could. And the Welshmen stopped playing jokes on their friends.

## STONE MOTHER—A PAIUTE LEGEND

The mother of the Paiute people had many children who did not get along. Their fighting led their father to separate them. The children he sent west became the Pitt River Indians. Those he sent east became the Bannocks. Those who stayed with their mother remained Paiute. She was very sad that her children had been separated. She cried as she sat on the mountains facing the Pitt River country where her children had gone. Her tears became a great lake now known as Pyramid Lake. In time, she yearned for her children so long that she turned to stone and is still there today, her basket by her side.

*The stone mother at Pyramid Lake is a legend of the Paiute people, who believe she will sit next to the lake forever.*

# Nevada's Sports Teams

**N**evada does not have any major-league professional sports teams. Instead, Nevadans cheer for college teams.

## COLLEGE TEAMS

College teams are very popular in Nevada. The University of Nevada, Las Vegas (UNLV), fans cheer for the Rebels. The Wolf Pack is the name of the University of Nevada, Reno (UNR), teams.

*In 2003 four Rebels soccer players were named to the all-Mountain West Conference team.*

Football has been well known at UNR, particularly during the 1940s and 1950s. One of the sport's most well-known players, Marion Motley, was inducted into the Football Hall of Fame. Several other players have been **Heisman Trophy** contenders, including Stan Heath (1948), Frank Hawkins (1981), and Trevor Insley (1999). Heath went on to play professional football with the Green Bay Packers, Hawkins with the Oakland and Los Angeles Raiders, and Insley with the Houston Texans.

In 2003, the UNLV's women's soccer team reached the semi-finals of the Mountain West Conference Tournament. A member of the team, Annii Magliulo, became the first player in school history to win all-region honors. She was named to the National Soccer Coaches Association West Region Team.

The men's basketball team at UNLV has been extremely successful, particularly in the 1980s. In the 1989–1990 season, the Rebels won the national championship. Greg Anthony, Stacey Augmon, David Butler, Anderson Hunt, and Larry Johnson made up the starting five. The team became so popular in Las Vegas that a new facility, the Thomas and Mack Center, was built for their games. Many UNLV players have gone on to play professional basketball.

*Like the UNLV Rebels, the Nevada Wolfpack have had success in the NCAA tournament. In 2004 the Wolfpack beat 2nd-seeded Gonzaga and advanced to the Sweet Sixteen.*

*Many women on the track and field team have hopes of someday competing in the Olympics.*

The women's track team is also sucessful at UNLV. The team has won many awards, and in 2003, thirteen team members—a record number—were named to the Academic All-Mountain West conference team. In 1998, a new track and field facility was built for the team. The team's coach, Barbara Edmonson, is not only an effective coach. As an athlete, she won a gold medal in the 1968 Olympics.

## FARM TEAMS

Las Vegas is home to a farm team of Major League Baseball's Los Angeles Dodgers. This team, the Las Vegas 51s, gets its name from a high security air force base called Area 51, located in the nearby Groom Mountains. The team plays in the sixteen-team Pacific Coast League. In 2003, the team had a 76–66 record. The 51s have won two Pacific Coast championships.

# Nevada's Businesses and Products

**T**oday, agriculture, ranching, and tourism are Nevada's major industries. Mining still plays an important role as well.

## AGRICULTURE AND RANCHING

About 6,800,000 acres of Nevada's land is used for growing crops and raising livestock. Agriculture is centered in communities such as Gardnerville, Minden, Moapa, Alamo, and the Amargosa Valley. In some areas, such as Fallon and Fernley, farmable soil has been created by irrigating the desert. One of the crops most suited to Nevada's dry climate is alfalfa hay, which is used to feed cattle and horses. Other important crops include cantaloupes, barley, potatoes, peppermint, timothy, sorghum, and oats. Dairy farms produce milk, cream, cottage cheese, and other dairy items.

*Most of Nevada's large cattle ranches are in the northern part of the state.*

The biggest agricultural industry in Nevada is livestock. Nevada's ranches are home to more than one-half million head of beef cattle. Other livestock raised on the state's ranches include sheep, pigs, rabbits, chickens, turkeys, and ducks. About 65 percent of Nevada's total income comes from the sale of livestock.

## MINING

Mining was once Nevada's most important industry, and the state was world-famous for its enormous gold and silver output. But by the mid-1900s, the importance of mining declined. In the 1960s, however, gold mining revived, and by the 1990s, Nevada was the nation's leading producer of gold as well as silver. By 2000, Nevada supplied 68 percent of the country's gold and 42 percent of its silver.

In 1975, the opening of the McDermitt mine in Humboldt County made Nevada become the nation's leading producer of mercury. Other minerals mined in the state include tungsten, iron ore, and lithium.

## A Day in the Life of a Miner

In the late 1800s and early 1900s, miners spent their days inside deep caves. Awakening at about 5:30 in the morning, miners started their work by 7:00. Swinging pickaxes and working by candlelight, the miners breathed hot, dust-filled air. At the same time, they listened closely for sounds that might warn them of a cave-in. After a brief break for lunch, the miners returned to the darkness of the mine—often until after dusk.

## TOURISM

Tourism is the biggest industry in Nevada, with about 47.5 million visitors each year. The state earns billions of dollars each year from tourist related spending and activities. Visitors come from across the United States, and about ten percent of the state's visitors, almost five million, are from other countries.

About 57 percent of Nevada's jobs are in the tourism industry or in businesses that support tourism. For example, people work as casino dealers, waiters, hotel and motel room workers, car parkers, cooks, and dishwashers. Other jobs related to tourism include car rental agents and airline employees, such as baggage handlers.

*With over 5,000 rooms, the MGM Grand is the largest hotel in the world. The MGM Grand, like other large hotels and casinos on the Vegas Strip, employs thousands of people in a variety of jobs.*

# Attractions and Landmarks

**A**lthough Las Vegas is Nevada's top tourist attraction, the state is filled with other human-made and natural attractions that visitors flock to see each year.

## HOOVER DAM

During the 1900s, the United States government built dams across the country to generate electricity, to irrigate land, and to control floods. One of the most famous dams ever built is Hoover Dam, known for its enormous size and for its graceful architecture.

### Building the Dam

Construction of the Hoover Dam began in 1931 and ended in 1936. At the time, there were no cities close to the building site. First, a railroad had to be built to bring supplies to the site. Then a temporary town was put up to provide homes for the workers. In all, about 5,000 people worked on the dam day and night during construction.

Hoover Dam is one of the largest structures the United States ever built. The dam stores water from the Colorado River and creates electricity for people in Arizona, Nevada, and California. A visitor center shows how the dam was built and how it works. Tour guides point out the special

*Boating is a popular activity with visitors at Lake Mead.*

design features of the dam and take visitors through the gigantic turbine engine areas where electricity is generated.

The damming of the Colorado River created Lake Mead, a large artificial lake used for swimming, fishing, boating, and water skiing. It attracts more than 10 million visitors each year. Lake Mead, with 550 miles of shoreline, covers 247 square miles, an area that is twice the size of Rhode Island.

## FORT CHURCHILL

Fort Churchill, Nevada's first and largest Army **fort,** operated for ten years, from 1860 until 1870. The fort

*Fort Churchill was a link in the transcontinental telegraph line, which was completed in 1861 and allowed people to send messages across the country quickly.*

# Places to See in Nevada

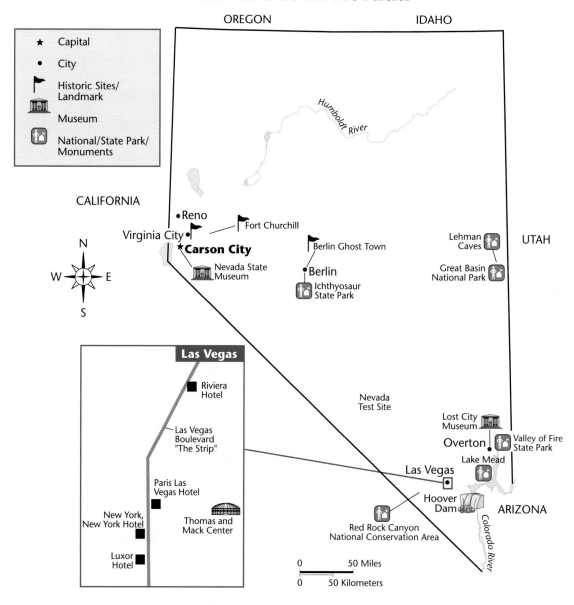

OREGON          IDAHO

Capital
City
Historic Sites/
Landmark
Museum
National/State Park/
Monuments

CALIFORNIA

Humboldt River

• Reno
Fort Churchill
Virginia City •
★ **Carson City**
Nevada State
Museum

Berlin Ghost Town

• Berlin
Ichthyosaur
State Park

Lehman
Caves

Great Basin
National Park

UTAH

N
W       E
S

**Las Vegas**

Riviera
Hotel

Las Vegas
Boulevard
"The Strip"

Nevada
Test Site

Lost City
Museum

Overton

Valley of Fire
State Park

Lake Mead

Las Vegas

Paris Las
Vegas Hotel

New York,
New York Hotel

Thomas and
Mack Center

Hoover
Dam

ARIZONA

Luxor
Hotel

Red Rock Canyon
National Conservation Area

Colorado River

0        50 Miles
0     50 Kilometers

was an important stop for settlers on their way west, and it also played a part in protecting the **Pony Express** mail route. Today, visitors can see the remains of many buildings that made up the fort.

## Carson City Mint

The Carson City Mint operated from 1870 until 1893, making gold and silver coins. Before the Carson City Mint opened, the gold and silver mined in Nevada had to be sent to San Francisco, California. Today, collectors prize the coins made at the Carson City mint. After the mint closed, it became the Nevada State Museum.

## Virginia City

Virginia City is a popular tourist attraction. After the Comstock Lode was discovered in 1859, people flocked to

*Parts of Virginia City have been damaged or burned, but people are rebuilding those places to look as they did in the 1800s.*

Virginia City, and its population soared to about 20,000 people. When the mining boom faded, most people left the city. However, others stayed and found new ways to make a living there. Today, the entire town of Virginia City is a National Historical Landmark, the largest one in the nation. Many places in the city look as they did in the 1800s. Tourists can visit museums, gift shops, the old opera house, historic churches, and **boot hills,** or they can take mine tours.

## GREAT BASIN NATIONAL PARK

Great Basin National Park was created so visitors would see the animals, plants, and geography of the area. Streams, lakes, forests, and limestone caverns are found in the park. Park visitors can hike, see the 5,000-year-old grove of bristlecone pine trees, observe birds and bats, visit the Lexington natural limestone arch, and view the Lehman caverns.

*The origins of the caves at Great Basin National Park can be traced back hundreds of millions of years to a time when Nevada was covered by an inland sea.*

## VALLEY OF FIRE

Dedicated in 1935, the Valley of Fire is Nevada's first state park. The valley's sandstone rock formations appear so red when the sunlight strikes them that they look as if they are on fire. Visitors also can see carvings made on some rocks by local people in about 1250, as well as petrified logs dating from **prehistoric** times. The formations are so striking that the Valley of Fire has been a favorite film location for movies such as *One Million B.C.*, *The Ballad of Cable Hogue*, and *Star Trek: Generations*.

## Lehman Caves— A Window to the Past

Lehman Caves are underground limestone caves in Great Basin National Park. Visitors may tour parts of the cave, seeing unique **stalactites** and **stalagmites,** formations in the caves that are made by mineral-filled droplets of water slowly dripping during hundreds or thousands of years. The caves became a national monument in 1922 and were incorporated into the Great Basin Park in 1986.

## LAKE TAHOE

Overlapping the Nevada-California border west of Carson City is Lake Tahoe, a mountain lake known for its alpine beauty. Covering an area 22 miles long and 12 miles wide, the lake is surrounded by lodges and picturesque beaches. A 150-mile-long hiking trail encircles the rim of the mountains that surround the lake basin. When the writer Mark Twain first saw Lake Tahoe in 1861, he wrote, "The lake burst upon us—a noble sheet of blue water lifted 6,300 feet above the level of the sea, and walled in by a rim of snow-clad mountain peaks that towered aloft 3,000 feet higher still! . . . As it lay there with the shadows of the mountains brilliantly photographed upon its still surface I thought it must surely be the fairest picture the whole earth affords."

*The Lake Tahoe area is a popular spot for hiking and water recreation in the summer and skiing in the winter.*

The lake and the surrounding area make it one of Nevada's most popular attractions.

## NEVADA TEST SITE

In 1951 the Department of Energy (DOE) established the Nevada Test Site to test nuclear weapons and the effects of radiation on the environment. The Test Site is located in the Nevada desert, 65 miles northwest of Las Vegas. Each month the DOE provides people the opportunity to see portions of the Test Site. Tour groups of about 10 people can take a 250-mile trip around the site to see the craters left by nuclear explosions and also learn about the peaceful uses for nuclear technology.

# Map of Nevada

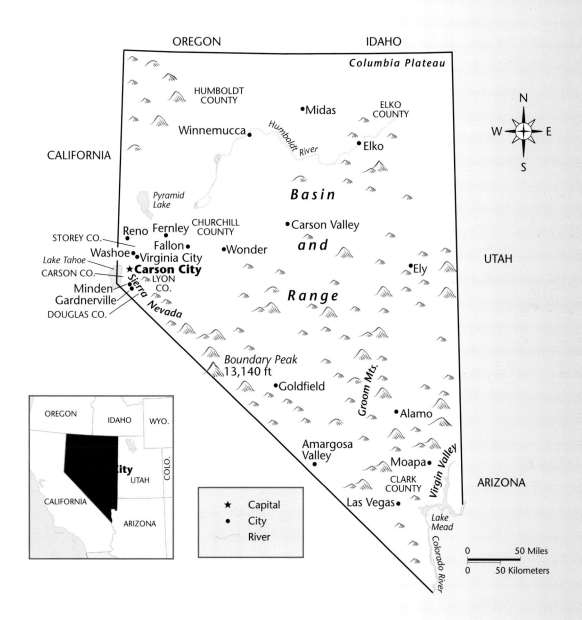

OREGON    IDAHO

Columbia Plateau

N
W E
S

HUMBOLDT
COUNTY

•Midas

ELKO
COUNTY

Winnemucca•

Humboldt River

•Elko

CALIFORNIA

*Basin*

Pyramid
Lake

STOREY CO.

Reno• Fernley•

CHURCHILL
COUNTY

•Carson Valley

*and*

Washoe•

Fallon•

•Wonder

•Ely

Lake Tahoe

•Virginia City

CARSON CO.

★**Carson City**

LYON
CO.

*Range*

UTAH

Minden•

Sierra Nevada

Gardnerville•

DOUGLAS CO.

Boundary Peak
13,140 ft

Groom Mts.

•Goldfield

•Alamo

Amargosa
Valley•

•Moapa

Virgin Valley

CLARK
COUNTY

ARIZONA

Las Vegas•

Lake
Mead

Colorado River

OREGON   IDAHO   WYO.

COLO.

...ity

UTAH

CALIFORNIA

ARIZONA

★   Capital
•   City
     River

0           50 Miles
0      50 Kilometers

# Glossary

**appeals**   court cases that the defendants ask a higher court to review

**Basque**   having to do with a people who live mainly in the Pyrenees Mountains of Spain and France and have their own distinct language

**boot hills**   cemeteries in the Old West where gunfighters were buried

**buttes**   steep hills with flat tops

**Civil War**   the war between the Union (the North) and the Confederacy (the South) in the U.S. (1861–1865) fought over issues such as states' rights and slavery

**ceded**   gave up control or possession of such things as land or trading rights, often as a result of a treaty

**census**   an official count of the number of people in the country, which is done every ten years in the United States

**federal government**   the government of the United States

**felony**   a serious crime, which is usually punishable by a penalty of more than one year in jail in addition to fines

**fort**   an army post

**ghost towns**   once-busy towns that have been abandoned

**glaciers**   thick, slow-moving sheets of ice

**Heisman Trophy**   an award given to the most-valuable college football player

**hydroelectric**   creating energy through the use of water power

**imps**   small demons

**lava**   liquid melted rock that rises from beneath the earth's surface and hardens when it cools

**majority**   a number more than one half of the total

**mesas**   large, flat areas on top of hills and mountains

**Paleolithic**   a cultural period lasting from about 750,000 years ago to about 15,000 years ago

**Pony Express**   a mail service in which riders on swift ponies carried and delivered the mail between Missouri and California (1860-1861)

**precipitation**   rain, sleet, or snow

**prehistoric**   belonging to a time period before events were written down

**prophet**   a person who can predict the future

**prospectors**   people who look for gold, silver, oil, or other minerals

**rain shadow**   the area on one side of a mountain range that receives little rain because the precipitation typically falls on the other side of the range

**ratified**   to have approved

**Reconstruction**   a period in United States history (1865–1877) in which the federal government tried to rebuild the South after the Civil War

**rodeo** a competition in which such skills as riding horses or roping calves are displayed and judged

**salt flats** a flat area of land with a salty surface, left behind by the evaporation of a body of water

**sickle** a curved blade used to cut tall grass or grain

**stalactites** mineral deposits projecting downward from the roof of a cave

**stalagmites** mineral deposits projecting upward from the floor of a cave

**trestle** a support to hold up a bridge

**vetoes** rejects a bill so that it cannot become a law without strong suport from the legislature (usually a two-thirds majority vote)

**Welsh** from or having to do with Wales in the United Kingdom

# More Books to Read

Carpenter, Allen. *The New Enchantment of America: Nevada,* Chicago: Children's Press, 1979.

Elliott, Russell. *History of Nevada,* Lincoln, Nebraska: University of Nebraska Press, 1973.

Hulse, James. *The Silver State,* Reno: University of Nevada Press, 1991.

Krummer, Patricia. *Nevada,* Minnesota: Capstone High/Low Books, 1999.

Stein, Conrad R. *Nevada: America the Beautiful, Second Series,* Chicago: Children's Press, 2000.

# Index

# About the Authors

Rebecca K. O'Connor lives in Southern California, near the deserts of Nevada. She has written children's books as well as adult fiction. She is one of the millions of people who visit Las Vegas every year.

Dennis Myers is a veteran Nevada journalist and writer. He is a former chief deputy secretary of state of Nevada.

D. J. Ross is a writer and educator with more than 30 years of experience in education. He frequently visits Nevada.